MW01600484

THE FOURTEEN BRAVEST CHRISTIANS

Did they die for a lie?

TODD BAUERLE

Scripture Attributions:

Unless otherwise noted, Scripture quotations are taken from the **King James Version (KJV)**, which is in the public domain.

Scripture quotations marked **(ESV)** are from *The Holy Bible, English Standard Version® (ESV®)*, copyright © 2001 by Crossway, a publishing ministry of Good News Publishers. Used by permission. All rights reserved.

Scripture quotations marked **(MSG)** or from *The Message* are from *The Message*, copyright © 1993, 2002, 2018 by Eugene H. Peterson. Used by permission of NavPress. All rights reserved. Represented by Tyndale House Publishers, Inc.

Scripture quotations marked **(NIV)** are from *The Holy Bible, New International Version®, NIV®*, copyright © 1973, 1978, 1984, 2011 by Biblica, Inc.™ Used by permission. All rights reserved worldwide.

Disclaimer:

This book is intended for educational and inspirational purposes only. The author has made every effort to ensure accuracy and clarity. However, readers are encouraged to consult the Bible and study resources personally to deepen their understanding.

TABLE OF CONTENTS

Introduction 1

Stephen, Ad 34 3

James, Aka "James The Great", Ad 44 7

Philip, Ad 54 11

Matthew, Ad 60 15

James The Less, Ad 63 19

John Mark, Ad 64 23

Simon Peter, Ad 69 29

Saul Paul, Ad 69 37

Matthias, Ad 70 51

Andrew, Ad 70 57

Judas Thaddaeus, Ad 70 61

Bartholomew/Nathaniel, Ad 70 65

Thomas, Ad 70 69

Simon The Zealot, Ad 74 75

Final Thoughts 79

Consider These Verses From The Message Bible (Msg) In The Book Of Matthew 23: 1-39: 80

Consider This Quote By Adam Kirsch: 89

The Difference Between A Disciple And A Follower 91

Order Of Disciples Called By Jesus 93

iii

Disciples Who Were Brothers... 93

Thirty-Seven Miracles Of Jesus In Chronological Order 94

References..**97**

INTRODUCTION

No one knows precisely whether it was a hot, balmy, or cool, blustery day on the northwest shore of the Galilee. There certainly seemed to be something different in the atmosphere. That certainly was true. Within a few years, life for those in that part of the world (and the whole world, for that matter) would change for all eternity, so much so that the calendar used to record history would be reset because of the events that unfolded. There was a young man walking among them. Rumors abounded regarding what He was saying and doing. His message and miracles are recorded in the best-selling book of all time. More importantly, the fourteen young men you are about to meet were eyewitnesses to His life from their meeting until His death. They actually walked, talked, and ate with Him before and after He came back from the dead. After He had been beaten almost to death, He was then nailed through His hands and feet to a cross to die (crucified). To prove He was dead, a Roman soldier pierced His pericardium (producing blood and water), indeed proving He was dead. These are the brief stories of the fourteen He trusted—who they were, what they witnessed, what they said, and how they died— all over 2,000 years ago.

Others also witnessed Jesus alive after His resurrection. I don't have the time to share their testimonies. By the way, these fourteen guys were likely between the ages of fifteen and thirty when they met Him; the custom of the day was for young men to be married by eighteen. Peter may have been the only one of the twelve disciples who was married at that time.

When I first read their accounts in [1]*Foxe's Book of Martyrs,* I had to bite my lip and wipe away burning tears. I had to stop reading often to figure out what to do with my emotions and ponder in awe at their bravery. I couldn't help being nervous, thinking about whether I would have been then, or would be now,

---

[1] Foxe, John. Foxe: Voices of the Martyrs. Salem Books, 2019.

brave enough to die for what I say to the world about who Jesus Christ is. Would I? I pray so!!

Mark 9:24 (NIV)

"24… I do believe; help me overcome my unbelief!"

1

STEPHEN, AD 34

WHO HE WAS

Stephen is not considered one of Jesus' twelve disciples, but he was, as far as we know, the first to be martyred for his belief in this man who was born in Bethlehem and raised in Nazareth and professed to be God Himself.

WHAT HE WITNESSED

Stephen likely witnessed or was told by those who did about Jesus turning water into wine at the wedding feast in Cana. *The following verses are taken from the New International Version (NIV):*

John 2:1-11

[1] On the third day a wedding took place at Cana in Galilee. Jesus' mother was there,

[2] and Jesus and his disciples had also been invited to the wedding.

[3] When the wine was gone, Jesus' mother said to him, "They have no

3

more wine." [4] "Woman, why do you involve me?" Jesus replied. "My hour has not yet come."

[5] His mother said to the servants, "Do whatever he tells you." Nearby stood six stone water jars, the kind used by the Jews for ceremonial washing, each holding from twenty to thirty gallons.

[7] Jesus said to the servants," Fill the jars with water"; so, they filled them to the brim.

[8] Then he told them, "Now draw some out and take it to the master of the banquet." They did so,

[9] and the master of the banquet tasted the water that had been turned into wine. He did not realize where it had come from, though the servants who had drawn the water knew. Then he called the bridegroom aside

[10] and said, "Everyone brings out the choice wine first and then the cheaper wine after the guests have had too much to drink; but you have saved the best till now."

[11] What Jesus did here in Cana of Galilee was the first of the signs through which he revealed his glory; and his disciples believed in him. He also likely saw Jesus heal a government official's son in the town of Capernaum, which sits on the shore of the Galilee.

John 4:43-54 (NIV)

[43] After the two days he left for Galilee.

[44] (Now Jesus himself had pointed out that a prophet has no honor in his own country.)

[45] When he arrived in Galilee, the Galileans welcomed him. They had seen all that he had done in Jerusalem at the Passover Festival, for they also had been there.

[46] Once more he visited Cana in Galilee, where he had turned the water into wine. And there was a certain royal official whose son lay

4

sick at Capernaum.

[47] When this man heard that Jesus had arrived in Galilee from Judea, he went to him and begged him to come and heal his son, who was close to death.

[48] "Unless you people see signs and wonders," Jesus told him, "You will never believe."

[49] The royal official said, "Sir, come down before my child dies."

[50] "Go," Jesus replied," your son will live." The man took Jesus at his word and departed.

[51] While he was still on the way, his servants met him with the news that his boy was living.

[52] When he inquired as to the time when his son got better, they said to him, "Yesterday, at one in the afternoon, the fever left him."

[53] Then the father realized that this was the exact time at which Jesus had said to him, "Your son will live." So, he and his whole household believed.

[54] This was the second sign Jesus performed after coming from Judea to Galilee.

WHAT HE SAID

Stephen sealed his fate with his fifty-verse blistering indictment of the religious elites, reminding them that from the earliest formation of Hebrew religious leadership, they had persecuted and tormented God's prophets and brought forth charges leading to their Messiah's (Jesus Christ's) crucifixion. You can read the details in Acts 7:2-53.

HOW HE DIED

Stephen was stoned to death, dying from blunt force trauma for refusing to denounce his belief in Jesus. Amid his stoning, he said:

Acts 7:56 (NIV)

[56] "Look," he said, "I see heaven open and the Son of Man standing at the right hand of God." And with his last breath, he said:

Acts 7:60 (NIV)

[60] "Then he fell on his knees and cried out, 'Lord, do not hold this sin against them.' When he had said this, he fell asleep."

2

JAMES, AKA "JAMES THE GREAT", AD 44

WHO HE WAS

James and his brother John were nicknamed "Boanerges" or "Sons of Thunder," because they were said to have had bold and aggressive personalities. He was also referred to as a son of Zebedee. Jesus called him off Zebedee's fishing boat. He was a fisherman. James and John's mother appealed to Jesus to favor her sons— here are her words:

Matthew 20:20-22 (NIV)

[20] Then the mother of Zebedee's sons came to Jesus with her sons and, kneeling down, asked a favor of him.

[21] "What is it" you want?" he asked. She said, "Grant that one of these two sons of mine may sit at your right and the other at your left in your king- dom."

[22] "You don't know what you are asking," Jesus said to them. "Can you drink the cup I am going to drink?" "We can," they answered.

7

WHAT HE WITNESSED

He saw Jesus drive out an evil spirit from a man in Capernaum.

Luke 4:31-36 (NIV)

^{31} Then he went down to Capernaum, a town in Galilee, and on the Sabbath he taught the people.

^{32} They were amazed at his teaching, because his words had authority.

^{33} In the synagogue there was a man possessed by a demon, an impure spirit. He cried out at the top of his voice,

^{34} "Go away! What do you want with us, Jesus of Nazareth? Have you come to destroy us? I know who you are—the Holy One of God!"

^{35} "Be quiet!" Jesus said sternly. "Come out of him!" Then the demon threw the man down before them all and came out without injuring him.

^{36} All the people were amazed and said to each other, "What words these are! With authority and power he gives orders to impure spirits and they come out!"

He also saw Jesus heal Peter's mother-in-law, who was sick with a fever:

Matthew 8:14-15 (NIV)

^{14} "When Jesus came into Peter's house, he saw Peter's mother-in-law lying in bed with a fever.

^{15} He touched her hand and the fever left her, and she got up and began to wait on him."

John 13:4-5 (NIV)

^{4} "I watched Jesus get up from the table at the Last Supper. He took

8

off His outer clothing and wrapped a towel around His waist.

^{5} After that, He poured water into a basin and began to wash my feet, drying them with the towel that was wrapped around Him."

WHAT HE SAID

There is nothing recorded in the Bible specifically attributed to something James said.

HOW HE DIED

James was beheaded in Jerusalem in AD 44, the first of the disciples to die, for refusing to denounce his belief in Jesus.

3

PHILIP, AD 54

WHO HE WAS

Philip came from the town of Bethsaida in Northern Israel, not far from Capernaum. He recruited his friend Nathanael to the cause and was the disciple who approached Jesus and told Him how much it would cost to feed the 5,000. He is believed to have taken the gospel to both Turkey and France, as they are now known. Philip was said to be multilingual and had an easy, outgoing personality.

WHAT HE WITNESSED

Obviously, he was with Jesus at the miracle of the feeding of the 5,000.

Mark 6:30-44 (NIV)

[30] The apostles gathered around Jesus and reported to him all they had done and taught.

[31] Then, because so many people were coming and going that they

11

did not even have a chance to eat, he said to them, "Come with me by yourselves to a quiet place and get some rest."

^{32} So they went away by themselves in a boat to a solitary place.

^{33} But many who saw them leaving recognized them and ran on foot from all the towns and got there ahead of them.

^{34} When Jesus landed and saw a large crowd, he had compassion on them, because they were like sheep without a shepherd. So, he began teaching them many things.

^{35} By this time it was late in the day, so his disciples came to him. "This is a remote place," they said, "and it's already very late.

^{36} Send the people away so that they can go to the surrounding countryside and villages and buy themselves something to eat."

^{37} But he answered, "You give them something to eat." They said to him, "That would take more than half a year's wages! Are we to go and spend that much on bread and give it to them to eat?"

^{38}"How many loaves do you have?" he asked. "Go and see." When they found out, they said, "Five—and two fish."

^{39} Then Jesus directed them to have all the people sit down in groups on the green grass.

^{40} So they sat down in groups of hundreds and fifties.

^{41} Taking the five loaves and the two fish and looking up to heaven, he gave thanks and broke the loaves. Then he gave them to his disciples to distribute to the people. He also divided the two fish among them all.

^{42} They all ate and were satisfied,

^{43} and the disciples picked up twelve basketfuls of broken pieces of bread and fish.

^{44} The number of the men who had eaten was five thousand.

He witnessed the first miraculous catch of fish on the Lake of Gennesaret,

AKA Sea of Galilee.

Luke 5:1-11 (NIV)

[1] One day as Jesus was standing by the Lake of Gennesaret, the people were crowding around him and listening to the word of God.

[2] He saw at the water's edge two boats, left there by the fishermen, who were washing their nets.

[3] He got into one of the boats, the one belonging to Simon, and asked him to put out a little from shore. Then he sat down and taught the people from the boat.

[4] When he had finished speaking, he said to Simon, "Put out into deep water, and let down the nets for a catch."

[5] Simon answered, "Master, we've worked hard all night and haven't caught anything. But because you say so, I will let down the nets."

[6] When they had done so, they caught such a large number of fish that their nets began to break.

[7] So they signaled their partners in the other boat to come and help them, and they came and filled both boats so full that they began to sink.

[8] When Simon Peter saw this, he fell at Jesus' knees and said, "Go away from me, Lord; I am a sinful man!"

[9] For he and all his companions were astonished at the catch of fish they had taken,

[10] and so were James and John, the sons of Zebedee, Simon's partners. Then Jesus said to Simon, "Don't be afraid; from now on you will fish for people."

[11] So they pulled their boats up on shore, left everything, and followed him.

13

I watched Jesus get up from the table at the Last Supper. He took off His outer clothing and wrapped a towel around His waist. After that, He poured water into a basin and began to wash my feet, drying them with the towel that was wrapped around Him.

WHAT HE SAID

He told Jesus the cost of feeding the 5,000, and asked Jesus, at the Last Supper, "Lord, show us the Father and it is sufficient for us period" (**John 14:8 NIV**).

HOW HE DIED

Philip was crucified and stoned. *Foxe's Book of Martyrs*[2] says, "Obviously, his executioners' tactics once again proved ineffective in stopping the gospel."

---

[2] Foxe, John. Foxe: Voices of the Martyrs. Salem Books, 2019.

4

MATTHEW, AD 60

WHO HE WAS

Matthew, also known as Levi, was a tax collector (making him despised in Capernaum). He was the only gospel author to record the account of Jesus' life in Hebrew. He is thought to have journeyed to Persia and Ethiopia in Africa.

WHAT HE WITNESSED

Jesus' cleansing a man with leprosy:

Matthew 8:1-4 (NIV)

[1] When Jesus came down from the mountainside, large crowds followed him.

[2] A man with leprosy came and knelt before him and said, "Lord, if you are willing, you can make me clean."

[3] Jesus reached out his hand and touched the man. "I am willing," he

15

said. "Be clean!" Immediately he was cleansed of his leprosy.

[4] Then Jesus said to him, "See that you don't tell anyone. But go, show yourself to the priest and offer the gift Moses commanded, as a testimony to them."

Jesus' healing of the Centurian's paralyzed servant in Capernaum:

Matthew 8:5-13 (NIV)

[5] When Jesus had entered Capernaum, a centurion came to him, asking for help.

[6] "Lord," he said, "my servant lies at home paralyzed, suffering terribly."

[7] Jesus said to him, "Shall I come and heal him?"

[8] The centurion replied, "Lord, I do not deserve to have you come under my roof. But just say the word, and my servant will be healed.

[9] For I myself am a man under authority, with soldiers under me. I tell this one, 'Go,' and he goes; and that one, 'Come,' and he comes. I say to my servant, 'Do this,' and he does it."

[10] When Jesus heard this, he was amazed and said to those following him, "Truly I tell you, I have not found anyone in Israel with such great faith.

[11] I say to you that many will come from the east and the west and will take their places at the feast with Abraham, Isaac, and Jacob in the kingdom of heaven.

[12] But the subjects of the kingdom will be thrown outside, into the darkness, where there will be weeping and gnashing of teeth."

[13] Then Jesus said to the centurion, "Go! Let it be done just as you believed it would." And his servant was healed at that moment.

16

Jesus' healing of a paralytic who was let down through the roof:

Luke 5:17-26 (NIV)

[17] One day Jesus was teaching, and Pharisees and teachers of the law were sitting there. They had come from every village of Galilee and from Judea and Jerusalem. And the power of the Lord was with Jesus to heal the sick.

[18] Some men came carrying a paralyzed man on a mat and tried to take him into the house to lay him before Jesus.

[19] When they could not find a way to do this because of the crowd, they went up on the roof and lowered him on his mat through the tiles into the middle of the crowd, right in front of Jesus.

[20] When Jesus saw their faith, he said, "Friend, your sins are forgiven."

[21] The Pharisees and the teachers of the law began thinking to themselves, "Who is this fellow who speaks blasphemy? Who can forgive sins but God alone?"

[22] Jesus knew what they were thinking and asked, "Why are you thinking these things in your hearts?

[23] Which is easier: to say, 'Your sins are forgiven,' or to say, 'Get up and walk'?

[24] But I want you to know that the Son of Man has authority on earth to forgive sins." So, he said to the paralyzed man, "I tell you, get up, take your mat and go home."

[25] Immediately, he stood up in front of them, took what he had been lying on, and went home praising God.

[26] Everyone was amazed and gave praise to God. They were filled with awe and said, "We have seen remarkable things today."

17

John 13:4-5 (NIV)

I watched Jesus get up from the table at the Last Supper. He took off His outer clothing and wrapped a towel around His waist. After that, He poured water into a basin and began to wash my feet, drying them with the towel that was wrapped around Him.

WHAT HE SAID

He wrote the Book of Matthew in the New Testament of the Bible.

HOW HE DIED

Matthew was pinned to the ground and beheaded in Naddaver, Ethiopia, in 70 AD.

5

JAMES THE LESS, AD 63

WHO HE WAS

Of the three James in the Bible, James, son of Alphaeus, was the least recognized. Little is recorded about him in the Gospel. It is tradition that he was assigned Syria as his mission field.

WHAT HE WITNESSED

Jesus' healing of a man's withered hand on the Sabbath:

Matthew 12:9-14 (NIV)

[9] Going on from that place, he went into their synagogue,

[10] and a man with a shriveled hand was there. Looking for a reason to bring charges against Jesus, they asked him, "Is it lawful to heal on the Sabbath?"

[11] He said to them, "If any of you has a sheep and it falls into a pit on the Sabbath, will you not take hold of it and lift it out?

19

[12] How much more valuable is a person than a sheep! Therefore, it is lawful to do good on the Sabbath."

[13] Then he said to the man, "Stretch out your hand." So he stretched it out and it was completely restored, just as sound as the other.

[14] But the Pharisees went out and plotted how they might kill Jesus.

Jesus' raising of a widow's son from the dead in Nain:

Luke 7:11-17 (NIV)

[11] Soon afterward, Jesus went to a town called Nain, and his disciples and a large crowd went along with him.

[12] As he approached the town gate, a dead person was being carried out—the only son of his mother, and she was a widow. And a large crowd from the town was with her.

[13] When the Lord saw her, his heart went out to her and he said, "Don't cry."

[14] Then he went up and touched the bier they were carrying him on, and the bearers stood still. He said, "Young man, I say to you, get up!"

[15] The dead man sat up and began to talk, and Jesus gave him back to his mother.

[16] They were all filled with awe and praised God. "A great prophet has appeared among us," they said. "God has come to help his people."

[17] This news about Jesus spread throughout Judea and the surrounding country.

John 13:4-5 (NIV)

I watched Jesus get up from the table at the Last Supper. He took off His outer clothing and wrapped a towel around His waist. After that,

20

He poured water into a basin and began to wash my feet, drying them with the towel that was wrapped around Him.

WHAT HE SAID

James preached the Gospel to the believers, transplanted Jews, and typical people living in the area known today as Syria.

HOW HE DIED

An account indicates that James may have been the first overseer of the church in Jerusalem. After returning from the mission field, when asked by the high priest to deny Jesus, he was taken to the highest point of the temple, where instead of denouncing his faith, he loudly proclaimed Jesus as the Messiah. He was thrown off the temple. The fall and stoning were said to have only broken his legs. He prayed on his knees, "Lord forgive them for they know not what they do." He was hit in the head with a stone and died in front of the entire crowd in Jerusalem, AD 63.

6

JOHN MARK, AD 64

WHO HE WAS

Mark may be best known for his writing in **Mark 14:51-52** (NIV):

^{51} "A young man, wearing nothing but a linen garment, was following Jesus. When they seized him,

^{52} he fled naked, leaving his garment behind." Mark's first missionary journey with Paul and Barnabas ended prematurely with him returning to Jerusalem. Later he was said to have traveled to Antioch, Babylon, and Rome. He was instrumental in founding and building the church in Alexandria, Egypt.

WHAT HE WITNESSED

Jesus' calming of the storm on the Sea of Galilee:

Mark 4:35-41 (NIV)

^{35} That day when evening came, he said to his disciples, "Let us go

23

over to the other side." [36] Leaving the crowd behind, they took him along, just as he was, in the boat. There were also other boats with him.

[37] A furious squall came up, and the waves broke over the boat, so that it was nearly swamped.

[38] Jesus was in the stern, sleeping on a cushion. The disciples woke him and said to him, "Teacher, don't you care if we drown?"

[39] He got up, rebuked the wind and said to the waves, "Quiet! Be still!" Then the wind died down and it was completely calm.

[40] He said to his disciples, "Why are you so afraid? Do you still have no faith?"

[41] They were terrified and asked each other, "Who is this? Even the wind and the waves obey him!"

Jesus' casting out the demon into a herd of pigs:

Mark 5:1-20 (NIV)

[1] They went across the lake to the region of the Gerasenes.

[2] When Jesus got out of the boat, a man with an impure spirit came from the tombs to meet him.

[3] This man lived in the tombs, and no one could bind him anymore, not even with a chain.

[4] For he had often been chained hand and foot, but he tore the chains apart and broke the irons on his feet. No one was strong enough to subdue him.

[5] Night and day among the tombs and in the hills he would cry out and cut himself with stones.

[6] When he saw Jesus from a distance, he ran and fell on his knees in front of him.

[7] He shouted at the top of his voice, "What do you want with me, Jesus, Son of the Most High God? In God's name don't torture me!"

[8] For Jesus had said to him, "Come out of this man, you impure spirit!"
[9] Then Jesus asked him, "What is your name?" "My name is Legion," he replied, "for we are many."

[10] And he begged Jesus again and again not to send them out of the area.

[11] A large herd of pigs was feeding on the nearby hillside.

[12] The demons begged Jesus, "Send us among the pigs; allow us to go into them."

[13] He gave them permission, and the impure spirits came out and went into the pigs. The herd, about two thousand in number, rushed down the steep bank into the lake and were drowned.

[14] Those tending the pigs ran off and reported this in the town and countryside, and the people went out to see what had happened.

[15] When they came to Jesus, they saw the man who had been possessed by the legion of demons, sitting there, dressed and in his right mind; and they were afraid.

[16] Those who had seen it told the people what had happened to the demon- possessed man—and told about the pigs as well.

[17] Then the people began to plead with Jesus to leave their region.

[18] As Jesus was getting into the boat, the man who had been demon-possessed begged to go with him.

[19] Jesus did not let him, but said, "Go home to your own people and tell them how much the Lord has done for you, and how he has had mercy on you."

[20] So the man went away and began to tell in the Decapolis how much Jesus had done for him. And all the people were amazed.

Jesus' healing of the woman in the crowd with an issue of blood:

Luke 8:40-48 (NIV)

[40] Now when Jesus returned, a crowd welcomed him, for they were all expecting him.

[41] Then a man named Jairus, a synagogue leader, came and fell at Jesus' feet, pleading with him to come to his house

[42] because his only daughter, a girl of about twelve, was dying. As Jesus was on his way, the crowds almost crushed him.

[43] And a woman was there who had been subject to bleeding for twelve years, but no one could heal her.

[44] She came up behind him and touched the edge of his cloak, and immediately her bleeding stopped.

[45] "Who touched me?" Jesus asked. When they all denied it, Peter said, "Master, the people are crowding and pressing against you."

[46] But Jesus said, "Someone touched me; I know that power has gone out from me."

[47] Then the woman, seeing that she could not go unnoticed, came trembling and fell at his feet. In the presence of all the people, she told them why she had touched him and how she had been instantly healed.

[48] Then he said to her, "Daughter, your faith has healed you. Go in peace."

John 13:4-5 (NIV)

I watched Jesus get up from the table at the Last Supper. He took off His outer clothing and wrapped a towel around His waist. After that, He poured water into a basin and began to wash my feet, drying them with the towel that was wrapped around Him.

26

WHAT HE SAID

He wrote the book of Mark in the New Testament of the Bible.

HOW HE DIED

Mark was captured by a mob in Alexandria, and using ropes possibly with hooks attached, they tied and dragged him over the cobblestone streets until he was torn apart but not dead. The next day, after the night in prison, he was again dragged through the streets until he died.

7

SIMON PETER, AD 69

WHO HE WAS

Brother of Andrew. Jesus named him Peter after the Greek word Petros, meaning "a piece of rock." For these years,

Peter was always by Jesus' side. Jesus told him he would now be a fisher of men, and he ministered in Babylon and Rome. He is probably best known for fulfilling Jesus' prophecy that he would deny Him three times before a cock crows. Peter did, but Jesus forgave him and fully reinstated him to his leadership position.

WHAT HE WITNESSED

Jesus' raising of Jarius' daughter back from being dead:

Mark 5: 21-24, 35-43 (NIV)

^{21} When Jesus had again crossed over by boat to the other side of the

29

lake, a large crowd gathered around him while he was by the lake.

[22] Then one of the synagogue leaders, named Jairus, came and when he saw Jesus, he fell at his feet.

[23] He pleaded earnestly with him, "My little daughter is dying. Please come and put your hands on her so that she will be healed and live."

[24] So Jesus went with him. A large crowd followed and pressed around him...

[35] While Jesus was still speaking, some people came from the house of Jairus, the synagogue leader. "Your daughter is dead," they said. "Why bother the teacher anymore?"

[36] Overhearing what they said, Jesus told him, "Don't be afraid; just believe."

[37] He did not let anyone follow him except Peter, James and John, the brother of James.

[38] When they came to the home of the syna- gogue leader, Jesus saw a commotion, with people crying and wailing loudly.

[39] He went in and said to them, "Why all this commotion and wailing? The child is not dead but asleep."

[40] But they laughed at him. After he put them all out, he took the child's father and mother and the disciples who were with him and went in where the child was.

[41] He took her by the hand and said to her, "Talitha koum!" (which means "Little girl, I say to you, get up!").

[42] Immediately, the girl stood up and began to walk around (she was twelve years old). At this they were completely astonished. [43] He gave strict orders not to let anyone know about this and told them to give her something to eat.

Jesus' healing of two blind men:

30

Matthew 9:27-31 (NIV)

[27] As Jesus went on from there, two blind men followed him, calling out, "Have mercy on us, Son of David!"

[28] When he had gone indoors, the blind men came to him, and he asked them, "Do you believe that I am able to do this?" "Yes, Lord," they replied.

[29] Then he touched their eyes and said, "According to your faith let it be done to you";

[30] and their sight was restored. Jesus warned them sternly, "See that no one knows about this." [31] But they went out and spread the news about him all over that region.

Jesus' healing of the man who was mute:

Matthew 9: 32-34 (NIV)

[32] While they were going out, a man who was demon-possessed and could not talk was brought to Jesus.

[33] And when the demon was driven out, the man who had been mute spoke. The crowd was amazed and said, "Nothing like this has ever been seen in Israel."

[34] But the Pharisees said, "It is by the prince of demons that he drives out demons."

John 13:4-5 (NIV)

I watched Jesus get up from the table at the Last Supper. He took off His outer clothing and wrapped a towel around His waist. After that, He poured water into a basin and began to wash my feet, drying them with the towel that was wrapped around Him.

31

John 6:68-69 (NIV)

[68] "Simon Peter answered him, 'Lord, to whom shall we go? You have the words of eternal life.

[69] We have come to believe and to know that you are the Holy One of God.'" He spoke often. It's recorded in the four Gospels, and he is the author of 1st and 2nd Peter in the New Testament.

At the Last Supper, the following dialogue took place between Jesus and Peter:

John 13:6-11 (NIV)

[6] He came to Simon Peter, who said to him, "Lord, are you going to wash my feet?"

[7] Jesus replied, "You do not realize now what I am doing, but later you will understand."

[8] "No," said Peter, "you shall never wash my feet." Jesus answered, "Unless I wash you, you have no part with me."

[9] "Then, Lord," Simon Peter replied, "not just my feet but my hands and my head as well!"

[10] Jesus answered, "Those who have had a bath need only to wash their feet; their whole body is clean. And you are clean, though not every one of you."

[11] For he knew who was going to betray him, and that was why he said not everyone was clean.

Later, during the dinner, this conversation took place between Jesus and Peter:

[31] When he was gone, Jesus said, "Now the Son of Man is glorified and God is glorified in him.

[32] If God is glorified in him, God will glorify the Son in himself and will glorify him at once.

[33] My children, I will be with you only a little longer. You will look for me, and just as I told the Jews, so I tell you now: 'Where I am going, you cannot come.

[34] A new command I give you: Love one another. As I have loved you, so you must love one another.'

[35] By this everyone will know that you are my disciples, if you love one another."

[36] Simon Peter asked him, "Lord, where are you going?" Jesus replied, "Where I am going, you cannot follow now, but you will follow later."

[37] Peter asked, "Lord, why can't I follow you now? I will lay down my life for you."

[38] Then Jesus answered, "Will you really lay down your life for me? Very truly I tell you, before the rooster crows, you will disown me three times!

This conversation between Jesus and Peter took place after Jesus' resurrection and miraculously providing a net-stretching 153 fish catch, the 3rd time He appeared to them since He was raised from the dead.

John 21:15-25 (NIV)

[15] When they had finished eating, Jesus said to Simon Peter, "Simon son of John, do you love me more than these?" "Yes, Lord," he said, "you know that I love you." Jesus said, "Feed my lambs."

[16] Again, Jesus said, "Simon, son of John, do you love me?" He answered, "Yes, Lord, you know that I love you." Jesus said, "Take

care of my sheep."

[17] The third time he said to him, "Simon, son of John, do you love me?" Peter was hurt because Jesus asked him the third time, "Do you love me?" He said, "Lord, you know all things; you know that I love you." Jesus said, "Feed my sheep.

[18] Very truly I tell you, when you were younger, you dressed yourself and went where you wanted; but when you are old, you will stretch out your hands, and someone else will dress you and lead you where you do not want to go."

[19] Jesus said this to indicate the kind of death by which Peter would glorify God. Then he said to him, "Follow me!"

[20] Peter turned and saw that the disciple whom Jesus loved was following them. (This was the one who had leaned back against Jesus at the supper and had said, "Lord, who is going to betray you?")

[21] When Peter saw him, he asked, "Lord, what about him?"

[22] Jesus answered, "If I want him to remain alive until I return, what is that to you? You must follow me."

[23] Because of this, the rumor spread among the believers that this disciple would not die. But Jesus did not say that he would not die; he only said, "If I want him to remain alive until I return, what is that to you?"

[24] This is the disciple who testifies to these things and who wrote them down. We know that his testimony is true.

[25] Jesus did many other things as well. If every one of them were written down, I suppose that even the whole world would not have room for the books that would be written.

HOW HE DIED

Peter spent months in prison throughout his life, and also near the end of his life. The Mamertine prison was known for its horrible conditions that could kill a prisoner alone. Though chained and tortured, Peter preached to his guards. He was eventually taken to the dungeon and then to Nero's circus, where he was crucified upside down because he didn't feel worthy to be crucified like Christ (head up).

SAUL PAUL, AD 69

WHO HE WAS

Saul, who became Paul after his encounter on the road to Damascus, was the chief antagonist and killer of Christians before his conversion. He was at Steven's stoning, encouraging it, and is believed to have written half of the New Testament writings, including Romans, 1 & 2 Corinthians, Galatians, Philippians, Colossians, 1 & 2 Thessalonians, 1 & 2 Timothy, Titus, Philemon, and Hebrews.

WHAT HE WITNESSED

Jesus' healing of an invalid in Bethesda:

John 5:1-15 (NIV)

[1] Some time later, Jesus went up to Jerusalem for one of the Jewish festivals.

[2] Now there is in Jerusalem near the Sheep Gate a pool, which in

Aramaic is called Bethesda and which is surrounded by five covered colonnades.

[3] Here, a great number of disabled people used to lie—the blind, the lame, the paralyzed.

[5] One who was there had been an invalid for thirty-eight years.

[6] When Jesus saw him lying there and learned that he had been in this condition for a long time, he asked him, "Do you want to get well?"

[7] "Sir," the invalid replied, "I have no one to help me into the pool when the water is stirred. While I am trying to get in, someone else goes down ahead of me."

[8] Then Jesus said to him, "Get up! Pick up your mat and walk."

[9] At once, the man was cured; he picked up his mat and walked. The day on which this took place was a Sabbath,

[10] and so the Jewish leaders said to the man who had been healed, "It is the Sabbath; the law forbids you to carry your mat."

[11] But he replied, "The man who made me well said to me, 'Pick up your mat and walk.'"

[12] So they asked him, "Who is this fellow who told you to pick it up and walk?"

[13] The man who was healed had no idea who it was, for Jesus had slipped away into the crowd that was there.

[14] Later, Jesus found him at the temple and said to him, "See, you are well again. Stop sinning, or something worse may happen to you."

[15] The man went away and told the Jewish leaders that it was Jesus who had made him well.

WHAT HE SAID

Paul in Jerusalem - Acts 22:1-30 (MSG)

[1-3] "My dear brothers and fathers, listen carefully to what I have to say before you jump to conclusions about me." When they heard him speaking Hebrew, they grew even quieter. No one wanted to miss a word of this. He continued, "I am a good Jew, born in Tarsus in the province of Cilicia, but educated here in Jerusalem under the exacting eye of Rabbi Gamaliel, thoroughly instructed in our religious traditions. And I've always been passionately on God's side, just as you are right now.

[4-5] "I went after anyone connected with this 'Way,' went at them with all my might, ready to kill for God. I rounded up men and women right and left and had them thrown in prison. You can ask the Chief Priest or anyone in the High Council to verify this; they all knew me well. Then I went off to our brothers in Damascus, armed with official documents authorizing me to hunt down the followers of Jesus there, arrest them, and bring them back to Jerusalem for sentencing.

[6-7] "As I arrived on the outskirts of Damascus about noon, a blinding light blazed out of the skies and I fell to the ground, dazed. I heard a voice: 'Saul, Saul, why are you out to get me?'

[8-9] "'Who are you, Master?' I asked.

"He said, 'I am Jesus the Nazarene, the One you're hunting down.' My companions saw the light, but they didn't hear the conversation.

[10-11] "Then I said, 'What do I do now, Master?'

"He said, 'Get to your feet and enter Damascus. There you'll be told everything that's been set out for you to do.' And so we entered Damascus, but nothing like the entrance I had planned—I was blind as a bat and my companions had to lead me in by the hand.

[12-13] "And that's when I met Ananias, a man with a sterling reputation in observing our laws—the Jewish community in Damascus is unanimous on that score. He came and put his arm on my shoulder.

'Look up,' he said. I looked and found myself looking right into his eyes—I could see again!

[14-16] "Then he said, 'The God of our ancestors has handpicked you to be briefed on his plan of action. You've actually seen the Righteous Innocent and heard him speak. You are to be a key witness to everyone you meet of what you've seen and heard. So what are you waiting for? Get up and get yourself baptized, scrubbed clean of those sins and personally acquainted with God.'

[17-18] "Well, it happened just as Ananias said. After I was back in Jerusalem and praying one day in the Temple, lost in the presence of God, I saw him, saw God's Righteous Innocent, and heard him say to me. 'Hurry up! Get out of here as quickly as you can. None of the Jews here in Jerusalem are going to accept what you say about me.'

[19-20] "At first I objected: 'Who has better credentials? They all know how obsessed I was with hunting out those who believed in you, beating them up in the meeting places and throwing them in jail. And when your witness Stephen was murdered, I was right there, holding the coats of the murderers and cheering them on. And now they see me totally converted. What better qualification could I have?'

[21] "But he said, 'Don't argue. Go. I'm sending you on a long journey to outsider non-Jews.'"

A Roman Citizen

[22-25] The people in the crowd had listened attentively up to this point, but now they broke loose, shouting out, "Kill him! He's an insect! Stomp on him!" They shook their fists. They filled the air with curses. That's when the captain intervened and ordered Paul to be taken into the barracks. By now the captain was thoroughly exasperated. He decided to interrogate Paul under torture in order to get to the bottom of this, to find out what he had done that provoked this outraged violence. As they spread-eagled him with strips of leather, getting him ready for the whip, Paul said to the centurion standing there, "Is

40

this legal: torturing a Roman citizen without a fair trial?"

[26] When the centurion heard that, he went directly to the captain. "Do you realize what you've done? This man is a Roman citizen!"

[27] The captain came back and took charge. "Is what I hear right? You're a Roman citizen?" Paul said, "I certainly am."

[28] The captain was impressed. "I paid a huge sum for my citizenship. How much did it cost you?"

"Nothing," said Paul. "It cost me nothing. I was free from the day of my birth."

[29] That put a stop to the interrogation. And it put the fear of God into the captain. He had put a Roman citizen in chains and come within a whisker of putting him under torture!

Before the High Council - Acts 23:1-11 (MSG)

[1-3] Paul surveyed the members of the council with a steady gaze, and then said his piece: "Friends, I've lived with a clear conscience before God all my life, up to this very moment." That set the Chief Priest Ananias off. He ordered his aides to slap Paul in the face. Paul shot back, "God will slap you down! What a fake you are! You sit there and judge me by the Law and then break the Law by ordering me slapped around!"

[4] The aides were scandalized: "How dare you talk to God's Chief Priest like that!"

[5] Paul acted surprised. "How was I to know he was Chief Priest? He doesn't act like a Chief Priest. You're right, the Scripture does say, 'Don't speak abusively to a ruler of the people.' Sorry."

[6] Paul, knowing some of the council was made up of Sadducees and others of Pharisees and how they hated each other, decided to exploit their antagonism: "Friends, I am a stalwart Pharisee

41

from a long line of Pharisees. It's because of my Pharisee convictions—the hope and resurrection of the dead—that I've been hauled into this court."

[7-9] The moment he said this, the council split right down the middle, Pharisees and Sadducees going at each other in heated argument. Sadducees have nothing to do with a resurrection or angels or even a spirit. If they can't see it, they don't believe it. Pharisees believe it all. And so a huge and noisy quarrel broke out. Then some of the religion scholars on the Pharisee side shouted down the others: "We don't find anything wrong with this man! And what if a spirit has spoken to him? Or maybe an angel? What if it turns out we're fighting against God?"

[10] That was fuel on the fire. The quarrel flamed up and became so violent the captain was afraid they would tear Paul apart, limb from limb. He ordered the soldiers to get him out of there and escort him back to the safety of the barracks.

A Plot Against Paul

[11] That night the Master appeared to Paul: "It's going to be all right. Everything is going to turn out for the best. You've been a good witness for me here in Jerusalem. Now you're going to be my witness in Rome!"

Festus Consults King Agrippa - Acts 25:13-27 (MSG)

[13-17] A few days later King Agrippa and his wife, Bernice, visited Caesarea to welcome Festus to his new post. After several days, Festus brought up Paul's case to the king. "I have a man on my hands here, a prisoner left by Felix. When I was in Jerusalem, the high priests and Jewish leaders brought a bunch of accusations against him and wanted me to sentence him to death. I told them that wasn't the way we Romans did

42

things. Just because a man is accused, we don't throw him out to the dogs. We make sure the accused has a chance to face his accusers and defend himself of the charges. So when they came down here I got right on the case. I took my place in the courtroom and put the man on the stand.

18-21 "The accusers came at him from all sides, but their accusations turned out to be nothing more than arguments about their religion and a dead man named Jesus, who the prisoner claimed was alive. Since I'm a newcomer here and don't understand everything involved in cases like this, I asked if he'd be willing to go to Jerusalem and be tried there. Paul refused and demanded a hearing before His Majesty in our highest court. So I ordered him returned to custody until I could send him to Caesar in Rome."

22 Agrippa said, "I'd like to see this man and hear his story."

"Good," said Festus. "We'll bring him in first thing in the morning and you'll hear it for yourself."

23 The next day everybody who was anybody in Caesarea found his way to the Great Hall, along with the top military brass. Agrippa and Bernice made a flourishing grand entrance and took their places. Festus then ordered Paul brought in.

24-26 Festus said, "King Agrippa and distinguished guests, take a good look at this man. A bunch of Jews petitioned me first in Jerusalem, and later here, to do away with him. They have been most vehement in demanding his execution. I looked into it and decided that he had committed no crime. He requested a trial before Caesar and I agreed to send him to Rome. But what am I going to write to my master, Caesar? All the charges made by the Jews were fabrications, and I've uncovered nothing else.

26-27 "That's why I've brought him before this company, and especially you, King Agrippa: so we can come up with

43

something in the nature of a charge that will hold water. For it seems to me silly to send a prisoner all that way for a trial and not be able to document what he did wrong."

"I Couldn't Just Walk Away" - Acts 26:1-32 (MSG)

[1-3] Agrippa spoke directly to Paul: "Go ahead—tell us about yourself."

Paul took the stand and told his story. "I can't think of anyone, King Agrippa, before whom I'd rather be answering all these Jewish accusations than you, knowing how well you are acquainted with Jewish ways and all our family quarrels.

[4-8] "From the time of my youth, my life has been lived among my own people in Jerusalem. Practically every Jew in town who watched me grow up—and if they were willing to stick their necks out they'd tell you in person—knows that I lived as a strict Pharisee, the most demanding branch of our religion. It's because I believed it and took it seriously, committed myself heart and soul to what God promised my ancestors—the identical hope, mind you, that the twelve tribes have lived for night and day all these centuries—it's because I have held on to this tested and tried hope that I'm being called on the carpet by the Jews. They should be the ones standing trial here, not me! For the life of me, I can't see why it's a criminal offense to believe that God raises the dead.

[9-11] "I admit that I didn't always hold to this position. For a time I thought it was my duty to oppose this Jesus of Nazareth with all my might. Backed with the full authority of the high priests, I threw these believers—I had no idea they were God's people!—into the Jerusalem jail right and left, and whenever it came to a vote, I voted for their execution. I stormed through their meeting places, bullying them into cursing Jesus, a one-

44

man terror obsessed with obliterating these people. And then I started on the towns outside Jerusalem.

12-14 "One day on my way to Damascus, armed as always with papers from the high priests authorizing my action, right in the middle of the day a blaze of light, light outshining the sun, poured out of the sky on me and my companions. Oh, King, it was so bright! We fell flat on our faces. Then I heard a voice in Hebrew: 'Saul, Saul, why are you out to get me? Why do you insist on going against the grain?'

15-16 "I said, 'Who are you, Master?'

"The voice answered, 'I am Jesus, the One you're hunting down like an animal. But now, up on your feet—I have a job for you. I've picked you to be my servant and witness to what's happened today and to what I am going to show you.

17-18 "'I'm sending you off to open the eyes of the outsiders so they can see the difference between dark and light, and choose light, see the difference between Satan and God, and choose God. I'm sending you off to present my offer of sins forgiven, and a place in the family, inviting them into the company of those who begin real living by believing in me.'

19-20 "What could I do, King Agrippa? I couldn't just walk away from a vision like that! I became an obedient believer on the spot. I started preaching this life-change—this radical turn to God and everything it meant in everyday life—right there in Damascus, went on to Jerusalem and the surrounding countryside, and from there to the whole world.

21-23 "It's because of this 'whole world' dimension that the Jews grabbed me in the Temple that day and tried to kill me. They want to keep God for themselves. But God has stood by me, just as he promised, and I'm standing here saying what I've been saying to anyone, whether king or child, who will listen.

And everything I'm saying is completely in line with what the prophets and Moses said would happen: One, the Messiah must die; two, raised from the dead, he would be the first rays of God's daylight shining on people far and near, people both godless and God-fearing."

[24] That was too much for Festus. He interrupted with a shout: "Paul, you're crazy! You've read too many books, spent too much time staring off into space! Get a grip on yourself, get back in the real world!"

[25-27] But Paul stood his ground. "With all respect, Festus, Your Honor, I'm not crazy. I'm both accurate and sane in what I'm saying. The king knows what I'm talking about. I'm sure that nothing of what I've said sounds crazy to him. He's known all about it for a long time. You must realize that this wasn't done behind the scenes. You believe the prophets, don't you, King Agrippa? Don't answer that—I know you believe."

[28] But Agrippa did answer: "Keep this up much longer and you'll make a Christian out of me!"

[29] Paul, still in chains, said, "That's what I'm praying for, whether now or later, and not only you but everyone listening today, to become like me—except, of course, for this prison jewelry!"

[30-31] The king and the governor, along with Bernice and their advisors, got up and went into the next room to talk over what they had heard. They quickly agreed on Paul's innocence, saying, "There's nothing in this man deserving prison, let alone death."

[32] Agrippa told Festus, "He could be set free right now if he hadn't requested the hearing before Caesar."

46

Here are some of the best quotes from Paul's writings from the New Testament in the King James Bible:

2 Corinthians 9:6

"But this I say, He which soweth sparingly shall reap also sparingly; and he which soweth bountifully shall reap also bountifully."

2 Corinthians 12:9–10

"And he said unto me, My grace is sufficient for thee: for my strength is made perfect in weakness. Most gladly therefore will I rather glory in my infirmities, that the power of Christ may rest upon me.

Therefore, I take pleasure in infirmities, in reproaches, in necessities, in persecutions, in distresses for Christ's sake: for when I am weak, then am I strong."

Philippians 3:14

"I press toward the mark for the prize of the high calling of God in Christ Jesus."

Philippians 4:11–13

"Not that I speak in respect of want: for I have learned, in whatsoever state I am, therewith to be content. I know both how to be abased, and I know how to abound: every where and in all things I am instructed both to be full and to be hungry, both to abound and to suffer need. I can do all things through Christ which strengtheneth me."

Romans 12:2

"And be not conformed to this world: but be ye transformed by the renewing of your mind, that ye may prove what is that good, and acceptable, and perfect, will of God."

Galatians 3:28

"There is neither Jew nor Greek, there is neither bond nor free, there is neither male nor female: for ye are all one in Christ Jesus."

47

Galatians 6:9–10

"And let us not be weary in well doing: for in due season we shall reap, if we faint not. As we have therefore opportunity, let us do good unto all men, especially unto them who are of the household of faith."

Romans 5:8

"But God commendeth his love toward us, in that, while we were yet sinners, Christ died for us."

2 Timothy 4:7–8

"I have fought a good fight, I have finished my course, I have kept the faith: Henceforth there is laid up for me a crown of righteousness, which the Lord, the righteous judge, shall give me at that day: and not to me only, but unto all them also that love his appearing."

1 Corinthians 13:4–8

"Charity suffereth long and is kind; charity envieth not; charity vaunteth not itself, is not puffed up, doth not behave itself unseemly, seeketh not her own, is not easily provoked, thinketh no evil; Rejoiceth not in iniquity, but rejoiceth in the truth; Beareth all things, believeth all things, hopeth all things, endureth all things. Charity never faileth: but whether there be prophecies, they shall fail; whether there be tongues, they shall cease; whether there be knowledge, it shall vanish away."

Philippians 4:19

"But my God shall supply all your need according to his riches in glory by Christ Jesus."

Romans 13:8

"Owe no man any thing, but to love one another: for he that loveth another hath fulfilled the law."

2 Corinthians 5:17

"Therefore, if any man be in Christ, he is a new creature: old things are passed away; behold, all things are become new."

Colossians 3:23–24

"And whatsoever ye do, do it heartily, as to the Lord, and not unto men; knowing that of the Lord ye shall receive the reward of the inheritance: for ye serve the Lord Christ."

1 Thessalonians 5:11
"Wherefore comfort yourselves together, and edify one another, even as also ye do."

Philippians 4:6–7

"Be careful for nothing; but in every thing by prayer and supplication with thanksgiving let your requests be made known unto God. And the peace of God, which passeth all understanding, shall keep your hearts and minds through Christ Jesus."

HOW HE DIED

Paul was beheaded outside the gate wall in Rome, in AD 69. He too refused to deny Jesus and His miracles.

9

MATTHIAS, AD 70

WHO HE WAS

Matthias was one of the alternates chosen to replace Judas after his betrayal and suicide. He is thought to have

been one of the seventy-two evangelists the Lord sent out.

As written by Luke, Luke 10:1-24 (NIV):

[1] After this the Lord appointed seventy-two others and sent them two by two ahead of him to every town and place where he was about to go.

[2] He told them, "The harvest is plentiful, but the workers are few. Ask the Lord of the harvest, therefore, to send out workers into his harvest field.

[3] Go! I am sending you out like lambs among wolves.

[4] Do not take a purse or bag or sandals; and do not greet anyone on the road.

51

[5] "When you enter a house, first say, 'Peace to this house.'

[6] If someone who promotes peace is there, your peace will rest on them; if not, it will return to you.

[7] Stay there, eating and drinking whatever they give you, for the worker deserves his wages. Do not move around from house to house.

[8] "When you enter a town and are welcomed, eat what is offered to you. [9] Heal the sick who are there and tell them, 'The kingdom of God has come near to you.'

[10] But when you enter a town and are not welcomed, go into its streets and say,

[11] 'Even the dust of your town we wipe from our feet as a warning to you. Yet be sure of this: The kingdom of God has come near.'

[12] I tell you; it will be more bearable on that day for Sodom than for that town.

[13] "Woe to you, Chorazin! Woe to you, Bethsaida! For if the miracles that were performed in you had been performed in Tyre and Sidon, they would have repented long ago, sitting in sackcloth and ashes.

[14] But it will be more bearable for Tyre and Sidon at the judgment than for you.

[15] And you, Capernaum, will you be lifted to the heavens? No, you will go down to Hades.

[16] "Whoever listens to you listens to me; whoever rejects you rejects me; but whoever rejects me rejects him who sent me."

[17] The seventy-two returned with joy and said, "Lord, even the demons submit to us in your name."

[18] He replied, "I saw Satan fall like lightning from heaven.

[19] I have given you authority to trample on snakes and scorpions and to overcome all the power of the enemy; nothing will harm you.

52

[20] However, do not rejoice that the spirits submit to you, but rejoice that your names are written in heaven."

[21] At that time Jesus, full of joy through the Holy Spirit, said, "I praise you, Father, Lord of heaven and earth, because you have hidden these things from the wise and learned, and revealed them to little children. Yes, Father, for this is what you were pleased to do.

[22] "All things have been committed to me by my Father. No one knows who the Son is except the Father, and no one knows who the Father is except the Son and those to whom the Son chooses to reveal him."

[23] Then he turned to his disciples and said privately, "Blessed are the eyes that see what you see.

[24] For I tell you that many prophets and kings wanted to see what you see but did not see it, and to hear what you hear but did not hear it."

He is believed to have traveled as far as the Black Sea, sharing the Gospel, but eventually returned to Jerusalem.

WHAT HE WITNESSED

Jesus walking on water.

Mark 6:45-52 (NIV)

[45] Immediately Jesus made his disciples get into the boat and go on ahead of him to Bethsaida, while he dismissed the crowd.

[46] After leaving them, he went up on a mountainside to pray.

[47] Later that night, the boat was in the middle of the lake, and he was alone on land.

[48] He saw the disciples straining at the oars, because the wind was against them. Shortly before dawn he went out to them, walking on the lake. He was about to pass by them,

53

[49] but when they saw him walking on the lake, they thought he was a ghost. They cried out,

[50] because they all saw him and were terrified. Immediately he spoke to them and said, "Take courage! It is I. Don't be afraid."

[51] Then he climbed into the boat with them, and the wind died down. They were completely amazed,

[52] for they had not understood about the loaves; their hearts were hardened.

Jesus' healing of many in Gennesaret that were sick, just by touching his garment.

Mark 6:53-56 (NIV)

[53] When they had crossed over, they landed at Gennesaret and anchored there.

[54] As soon as they got out of the boat, people recognized Jesus.

[55] They ran throughout that whole region and carried the sick on mats to wherever they heard he was.

[56] And wherever he went—into villages, towns or countryside—they placed the sick in the marketplaces. They begged him to let them touch even the edge of his cloak, and all who touched it were healed.

WHAT HE SAID

Little is noted in the Bible regarding Matthias' words.

HOW HE DIED

He was stoned to death for refusing to sacrifice to the god, Jupiter. Another theory stated that he was hanged on a cross, stoned, and then beheaded with an ax for blaspheming God, Moses, and the Law. He was said to have said, "Thy blood be upon thy head, for thine own mouth has spoken against thee."

10

ANDREW, AD 70

WHO HE WAS

Simon Peter's brother first followed John the Baptist. In fact, he was standing with John the Baptist when he identified Jesus to a crowd, as the one he had been preaching about. He was a great connector, a center of influence in today's jargon. His missionary journeys took him to Southern Russia, Ephesus, ending in Greece in the City of Petras.

WHAT HE WITNESSED

Jesus healed the demon-possessed daughter of a gentile woman.

Matthew 15:21-28 (NIV)

^{21} Leaving that place, Jesus withdrew to the region of Tyre and Sidon.

^{22} A Canaanite woman from that vicinity came to him, crying out, "Lord, Son of David, have mercy on me! My daughter is demon-possessed and suffering terribly."

57

[23] Jesus did not answer a word. So, his disciples came to him and urged him, "Send her away, for she keeps crying out after us."

[24] He answered, "I was sent only to the lost sheep of Israel."

[25] The woman came and knelt before him. "Lord, help me!" she said.

[26] He replied, "It is not right to take the children's bread and toss it to the dogs."

[27] "Yes, it is, Lord," she said. "Even the dogs eat the crumbs that fall from their master's table."

[28] Then Jesus said to her, "Woman, you have great faith! Your request is granted." And her daughter was healed at that moment.

Jesus' healing of the deaf and dumb man:

Mark 7:31-37 (NIV)

[31] Then Jesus left the vicinity of Tyre and went through Sidon, down to the Sea of Galilee and into the region of the Decapolis.

[32] There some people brought to him a man who was deaf and could hardly talk, and they begged Jesus to place his hand on him.

[33] After he took him aside, away from the crowd, Jesus put his fingers into the man's ears. Then he spit and touched the man's tongue.

[34] He looked up to heaven and with a deep sigh said to him, "Ephphatha!" (which means "Be opened!").

[35] At this, the man's ears were opened, his tongue was loosened, and he began to speak plainly.

[36] Jesus commanded them not to tell anyone. But the more he did so, the more they kept talking about it.

[37] People were overwhelmed with amazement. "He has done everything well," they said. "He even makes the deaf hear and the

mute speak."

Jesus' feeding of the 4,000, in addition to all the women and children:

Mark 8:1-13 (NIV)

[1] During those days, another large crowd gathered. Since they had nothing to eat, Jesus called his disciples to him and said,

[2] "I have compassion for these people; they have already been with me three days and have nothing to eat.

[3] If I send them home hungry, they will collapse on the way, because some of them have come a long distance."

[4] His disciples answered, "But where in this remote place can anyone get enough bread to feed them?"

[5] "How many loaves do you have?" Jesus asked. "Seven," they replied.

[6] He told the crowd to sit down on the ground. When he had taken the seven loaves and given thanks, he broke them and gave them to his disciples to distribute to the people, and they did so.

[7] They had a few small fish as well; he gave thanks for them also and told the disciples to distribute them.

[8] The people ate and were satisfied. Afterward the disciples picked up seven basketfuls of broken pieces that were left over.

[9] About four thou- sand were present. After he had sent them away,

[10] he got into the boat with his disciples and went to the region of Dalmanutha.

[11] The Pharisees came and began to question Jesus. To test him, they asked him for a sign from heaven.

[12] He sighed deeply and said, "Why does this generation ask for a sign? Truly I tell you, no sign will be given to it."

[13] Then he left them, got back into the boat and crossed to the other side.

John 13:4-5 (NIV)

I watched Jesus get up from the table at the Last Supper. He took off His outer clothing and wrapped a towel around His waist. After that, He poured water into a basin and began to wash my feet, drying them with the towel that was wrapped around Him.

WHAT HE SAID

According to **John 6:4-13**, Andrew was the disciple who spoke to the young boy with the five loaves and two fish.

HOW HE DIED

He was threatened with crucifixion by the Roman governor for converting his wife. Andrew replied, "Had I feared the death of the cross, I should not have preached the majesty and gloriousness of Christ."

Refusing to denounce his faith in Christ, he was tied to an "X" shaped cross and died a slow, painful death. It is reported that as Andrew approached the cross, he said, *"Oh beloved cross! I have greatly longed for thee. I rejoice to see thee erected here, I come to thee with peaceful conscience and with cheerfulness, desiring that I, who am a disciple of Him who hung on the cross, may also be crucified. The nearer I come to the cross, the nearer I come to God, and the farther I am from the cross, the farther I remain from God."*

He hung for three days, reportedly saying, *"I thank my lord Jesus Christ, that he, having used me for a time as an ambassador, now permits me to have this body, that I, through the good confession, may obtain everlasting grace and mercy. Remain steadfast in the word and doctrine which you have received, instructing one another, that you may dwell with God in eternity, and receive the fruit of His promises."*

11

JUDAS THADDAEUS, AD 70

WHO HE WAS

Known as Judas the Faithful, son of James, not to be confused with Judas Iscariot, Jesus' betrayer. He ministered in the region of the Caspian Sea and was instrumental in Armenia becoming the first Christian nation in the fourth century.

WHAT HE WITNESSED

Jesus' healing of the blind man in Bethsaida:

Mark 8:22-26 (NIV)

22 They came to Bethsaida, and some people brought a blind man and begged Jesus to touch him.

23 He took the blind man by the hand and led him outside the village. When he had spit on the man's eyes and put his hands on him, Jesus asked, "Do you see anything?"

61

[24] He looked up and said, "I see people; they look like trees walking around."

[25] Once more Jesus put his hands on the man's eyes. Then his eyes were opened, his sight was restored, and he saw everything clearly.

[26] Jesus sent him home, saying, "Don't even go into the village."

Jesus' spitting in the eyes of the man blind from birth, restoring his sight:

John 9: 1-7 (NIV)

[1] As he went along, he saw a man blind from birth.

[2] His disciples asked him, "Rabbi, who sinned, this man or his parents, that he was born blind?"

[3] "Neither this man nor his parents sinned," said Jesus, "but this happened so that the works of God might be displayed in him.

[4] As long as it is day, we must do the works of him who sent me. Night is coming when no one can work.

[5] While I am in the world, I am the light of the world."

[6] After saying this, he spit on the ground, made some mud with the saliva, and put it on the man's eyes.

[7] "Go," he told him, "wash in the Pool of Siloam" (this word means "Sent"). So, the man went and washed, and came home seeing.

Jesus' casting out the unclean spirit, healing a young boy:

Mark 9:14-29 (NIV)

[14] When they came to the other disciples, they saw a large crowd around them and the teachers of the law arguing with them.

[15] As soon as all the people saw Jesus, they were overwhelmed with

wonder and ran to greet him.

[16] "What are you arguing with them about?" he asked.

[17] A man in the crowd answered, "Teacher, I brought you my son, who is possessed by a spirit that has robbed him of speech.

[18] Whenever it seizes him, it throws him to the ground. He foams at the mouth, gnashes his teeth, and becomes rigid. I asked your disciples to drive out the spirit, but they could not."

[19] "You unbelieving generation," Jesus replied, "how long shall I stay with you? How long shall I put up with you? Bring the boy to me."

[20] So they brought him. When the spirit saw Jesus, it immediately threw the boy into a convulsion. He fell to the ground and rolled around, foaming at the mouth.

[21] Jesus asked the boy's father, "How long has he been like this?" "From childhood," he answered.

[22] "It has often thrown him into fire or water to kill him. But if you can do anything, take pity on us and help us."

[23] "'If you can?'" said Jesus. "Everything is possible for one who believes."

[24] Immediately, the boy's father exclaimed, "I do believe; help me overcome my unbelief!"

[25] When Jesus saw that a crowd was running to the scene, he rebuked the impure spirit. "You deaf and mute spirit," he said, "I command you, come out of him and never enter him again."

[26] The spirit shrieked, convulsed him violently, and came out. The boy looked so much like a corpse that many said, "He's dead."

[27] But Jesus took him by the hand and lifted him to his feet, and he stood up. [28] After Jesus had gone indoors, his disciples asked him privately, "Why couldn't we drive it out?" [29] He replied, "This kind can come out only by prayer."

I watched Jesus get up from the table at the Last Supper. He took off His outer clothing and wrapped a towel around His waist. After that, He poured water into a basin and began to wash my feet, drying them with the towel that was wrapped around Him.

WHAT HE SAID

Little is recorded about his speaking. However, he did ask Jesus, "Lord, how is it that You will manifest Yourself to us, and not to the world?" His question basically was, "How can You rule the world and not show Yourself to the world?"

HOW HE DIED

He was martyred by arrow and javelin, in AD 70.

12

BARTHOLOMEW/ NATHANIEL, AD 70

WHO HE WAS

Bartholomew is best known for his comment to Philip, who introduced him to Jesus, "Can anything good come out of Nazareth?" He, like Judas, ministered in Armenia.

WHAT HE WITNESSED

Jesus providing the temple tax from a coin in the mouth of a fish:

Matthew 17:24-27 (NIV)

^{24} After Jesus and his disciples arrived in Capernaum, the collectors of the two-drachma temple tax came to Peter and asked, "Doesn't your teacher pay the temple tax?"

^{25} "Yes, he does," he replied. When Peter came into the house, Jesus was the first to speak. "What do you think, Simon?" he asked. "From

65

whom do the kings of the earth collect duty and taxes—from their own children or from others?"

[26] "From others," Peter answered. "Then the children are exempt," Jesus said to him.

[27] "But so that we may not cause offense, go to the lake and throw out your line. Take the first fish you catch; open its mouth and you will find a four-drachma coin. Take it and give it to them for my tax and yours."

Jesus' healing of the blind, mute, demoniac:

Matthew 21:22-23 (NIV)

[22] Then they brought him a demon-possessed man who was blind and mute, and Jesus healed him, so that he could both talk and see.

[23] All the people were astonished and said, "Could this be the Son of David?"

Jesus' healing of the woman crippled for 18 years:

Luke 13:10-17 (NIV)

[10] On a Sabbath Jesus was teaching in one of the synagogues,

[11] and a woman was there who had been crippled by a spirit for eighteen years. She was bent over and could not straighten up at all.

[12] When Jesus saw her, he called her forward and said to her, "Woman, you are set free from your infirmity."

[13] Then he put his hands on her, and immediately she straightened up and praised God.

[14] Indignant because Jesus had healed on the Sabbath, the synagogue leader said to the people, "There are six days for work. So come and be healed on those days, not on the Sabbath."

[15] The Lord answered him, "You hypocrites! Doesn't each of you on the Sabbath untie your ox or donkey from the stall and lead it out to give it water?

[16] Then should not this woman, a daughter of Abraham, whom Satan has kept bound for eighteen long years, be set free on the Sabbath day from what bound her?"

[17] When he said this, all his opponents were humiliated, but the people were delighted with all the wonderful things he was doing.

John 13:4-5 (NIV)

I watched Jesus get up from the table at the Last Supper. He took off His outer clothing and wrapped a towel around His waist. After that, He poured water into a basin and began to wash my feet, drying them with the towel that was wrapped around Him.

WHAT HE SAID

Other than his snide remark about anything good coming out of Nazareth, his first interaction with Jesus produced this dialogue:

Jesus: "Behold an Israelite indeed, in whom there is no deceit."
Bartholome: "How do you know me?"

"Then Nathanael declared, 'Rabbi, you are the Son of God; you are the king of Israel.'" **(John 1:49, NIV).**

HOW HE DIED

He was flayed and whipped until virtually all his skin fell from his body. Then crucified, possibly upside down. A martyr for Christ around AD 70.

13

THOMAS, AD 70

WHO HE WAS

Thomas is best known for his doubt that Jesus was alive. He was not with the other disciples on Sunday night when Jesus appeared to them.

WHAT HE WITNESSED

Jesus's healing on the Sabbath, the man with dropsy:

Luke 14:1-6 (NIV)

[1] One Sabbath, when Jesus went to eat in the house of a prominent Pharisee, he was being carefully watched.

[2] There in front of him was a man suffering from abnormal swelling of his body.

[3] Jesus asked the Pharisees and experts in the law, "Is it lawful to heal on the Sabbath or not?"

[4] But they remained silent. So, taking hold of the man, he healed him

and sent him on his way.

[5] Then he asked them, "If one of you has a child or an ox that falls into a well on the Sabbath day, will you not immediately pull it out?"

[6] And they had nothing to say.

Jesus' cleansing of the ten lepers:

Luke 17:11-19 (NIV)

[11] Now on his way to Jerusalem, Jesus traveled along the border between Samaria and Galilee.

[12] As he was going into a village, ten men who had leprosy met him. They stood at a distance

[13] and called out in a loud voice, "Jesus, Master, have pity on us!"

[14] When he saw them, he said, "Go, show yourselves to the priests." And as they went, they were cleansed.

[15] One of them, when he saw he was healed, came back, praising God in a loud voice.

[16] He threw himself at Jesus' feet and thanked him, and he was a Samaritan.

[17] Jesus asked, "Were not all ten cleansed? Where are the other nine?

[18] Has no one returned to give praise to God except this foreigner?"

[19] Then he said to him, "Rise and go; your faith has made you well."

Jesus raising his friend, Mary and Martha's brother, Lazarus, from being dead for three days:

John 11:1-45 (NIV)

[1] Now, a man named Lazarus was sick. He was from Bethany, the

70

village of Mary and her sister Martha.

[2] (This Mary, whose brother Lazarus now lay sick, was the same one who poured perfume on the Lord and wiped his feet with her hair.)

[3] So the sisters sent word to Jesus, "Lord, the one you love is sick."

[4] When he heard this, Jesus said, "This sickness will not end in death. No, it is for God's glory so that God's Son may be glorified through it."

[5] Now Jesus loved Martha and her sister and Lazarus.

[6] So when he heard that Lazarus was sick, he stayed where he was two more days,

[7] and then he said to his disciples, "Let us go back to Judea."

[8] "But Rabbi," they said, "a short while ago the Jews there tried to stone you, and yet you are going back?"

[9] Jesus answered, "Are there not twelve hours of daylight? Anyone who walks in the daytime will not stumble, for they see by this world's light.

[10] It is when a person walks at night that they stumble, for they have no light.

[11] After he had said this, he went on to tell them, "Our friend Lazarus has fallen asleep; but I am going there to wake him up."

[12] His disciples replied, "Lord, if he sleeps, he will get better."

[13] Jesus had been speaking of his death, but his disciples thought he meant natural sleep.

[14] So then he told them plainly, "Lazarus is dead,

[15] and for your sake I am glad I was not there, so that you may believe. But let us go to him."

[16] Then Thomas (also known as Didymus) said to the rest of the disciples, "Let us also go, that we may die with him."

71

[17] On his arrival, Jesus found that Lazarus had already been in the tomb for four days.

[18] Now Bethany was less than two miles from Jerusalem,

[19] and many Jews had come to Martha and Mary to comfort them in the loss of their brother.

[20] When Martha heard that Jesus was coming, she went out to meet him, but Mary stayed at home.

[21] "Lord," Martha said to Jesus, "if you had been here, my brother would not have died.

[22] But I know that even now God will give you whatever you ask."

[23] Jesus said to her, "Your brother will rise again."

[24] Martha answered, "I know he will rise again in the resurrection at the last day."

[25] Jesus said to her, "I am the resurrection and the life. The one who believes in me will live, even though they die;

[26] and whoever lives by believing in me will never die. Do you believe this?"

[27] "Yes, Lord," she replied, "I believe that you are the Messiah, the Son of God, who is to come into the world."

[28] After she had said this, she went back and called her sister Mary aside. "The Teacher is here," she said, "and is asking for you."

[29] When Mary heard this, she got up quickly and went to him.

[30] Now Jesus had not yet entered the village but was still at the place where Martha had met him.

[31] When the Jews who had been with Mary in the house, comforting her, noticed how quickly she got up and went out, they followed her, supposing she was going to the tomb to mourn there.

[32] When Mary reached the place where Jesus was and saw him, she

72

fell at his feet and said, "Lord, if you had been here, my brother would not have died."

[33] When Jesus saw her weeping, and the Jews who had come along with her also weeping, he was deeply moved in spirit and troubled.

[34] "Where have you laid him?" he asked. "Come and see, Lord," they replied.

[35] Jesus wept.

[36] Then the Jews said, "See how he loved him!"

[37] But some of them said, "Could not he who opened the eyes of the blind man have kept this man from dying?"

[38] Jesus, once more deeply moved, came to the tomb. It was a cave with a stone laid across the entrance.

[39] "Take away the stone," he said. "But, Lord," said Martha, the sister of the dead man, "by this time there is a bad odor, for he has been there four days."

[40] Then Jesus said, "Did I not tell you that if you believe, you will see the glory of God?"

[41] So they took away the stone. Then Jesus looked up and said, "Father, I thank you that you have heard me.

[42] I knew that you always hear me, but I said this for the benefit of the people standing here, that they may believe that you sent me."

[43] When he had said this, Jesus called in a loud voice, "Lazarus, come out!"

[44] The dead man came out, his hands and feet wrapped with strips of linen, and a cloth around his face. Jesus said to them, "Take off the grave clothes and let him go."

[45] Therefore many of the Jews who had come to visit Mary, and had seen what Jesus did, believed in him.

I watched Jesus get up from the table at the Last Supper. He took off His outer clothing and wrapped a towel around His waist. After that, He poured water into a basin and began to wash my feet, drying them with the towel that was wrapped around Him.

WHAT HE SAID

He said, *"Unless I see in his hands the print of the nails and put my finger into the print of his of his of the nails, and put my hand into his side, I will not believe."* About a week later, Jesus appeared to Thomas.

His doubts evaporated immediately when Thomas placed his hand inside Jesus' wounds, and he responded, "My Lord and my God! This is used in liturgical church services the world over to this day.

HOW HE DIED

A martyr tortured, thrown into an oven, and speared to death in Calamina, India, in AD 70. His tomb can be visited today in Mylapore, India.

14

SIMON THE ZEALOT, AD 74

WHO HE WAS

Known as an overt hater of Rome and its rule. An activist was likely hoping that Jesus would usher in a new Kingdom, thus abolishing Roman rule. He tried to avoid the spotlight. His travels took him across northern Africa, passing through Egypt and Libya, Mauritania, then to Spain, and finally Britain. He ended his life in the Middle East, possibly Persia.

WHAT HE WITNESSED

Jesus, in Jericho, restoring Bartimaeus' sight:

Mark 10:46-52 (NIV)

46 Then they came to Jericho. As Jesus and his disciples, together with a large crowd, were leaving the city, a blind man, Bartimaeus (which means "son of Timaeus"), was sitting by the roadside begging.

47 When he heard that it was Jesus of Nazareth, he began to shout, "Jesus, Son of David, have mercy on me!"

[48] Many rebuked him and told him to be quiet, but he shouted all the more, "Son of David, have mercy on me!"

[49] Jesus stopped and said, "Call him." So, they called to the blind man, "Cheer up! On your feet! He's calling you."

[50] Throwing his cloak aside, he jumped to his feet and came to Jesus.

[51] "What do you want me to do for you?" Jesus asked him. The blind man said, "Rabbi, I want to see."

[52] "Go," said Jesus, "your faith has healed you." Immediately, he received his sight and followed Jesus along the road.

Jesus, on the road from Bethany, withering the fig tree:

Matthew 21:18-22 (NIV)

[18] Early in the morning, as Jesus was on his way back to the city, he was hungry.

[19] Seeing a fig tree by the road, he went up to it but found nothing on it except leaves. Then he said to it, "May you never bear fruit again!" Immediately, the tree withered.

[20] When the disciples saw this, they were amazed. "How did the fig tree wither so quickly?" they asked.

[21] Jesus replied, "Truly I tell you, if you have faith and do not doubt, not only can you do what was done to the fig tree, but also you can say to this mountain, 'Go, throw yourself into the sea,' and it will be done.

[22] If you believe, you will receive whatever you ask for in prayer."

Jesus, while being arrested, heals the soldier's severed ear:

Luke 22:50-51 (NIV)

[50] "And one of them struck the servant of the high priest, cutting off his right ear.

[51] But Jesus answered, 'No more of this!' And he touched the man's ear and healed him."

Jesus facilitating the second miraculous netting of fish in the Sea of Tiberias (AKA Sea of Galilee):

John 21:4-11 (NIV)

[4] Early in the morning, Jesus stood on the shore, but the disciples did not realize that it was Jesus.

[5] He called out to them, "Friends, haven't you any fish?" "No," they answered.

[6] He said, "Throw your net on the right side of the boat and you will find some." When they did, they were unable to haul the net in because of the large number of fish.

[7] Then the disciple whom Jesus loved said to Peter, "It is the Lord!" As soon as Simon Peter heard him say, "It is the Lord," he wrapped his outer garment around him (for he had taken it off) and jumped into the water.

[8] The other disciples followed in the boat, towing the net full of fish, for they were not far from shore, about a hundred yards.

[9] When they landed, they saw a fire of burning coals there with fish on it, and some bread.

[10] Jesus said to them, "Bring some of the fish you have just caught."

[11] So Simon Peter climbed back into the boat and dragged the net ashore. It was full of large fish, 153, but even with so many, the net was not torn.

77

WHAT HE SAID

There is very little written in the Gospels regarding Simon. That may be because he kept a low profile after being a zealous antagonist to the Roman authorities before his affiliation with Jesus.

HOW HE DIED

Simon was sawed in half for his belief in Jesus Christ, AD 74.

FINAL THOUGHTS

Neither John, the disciple Jesus loved, nor Luke, a major contributor to the Gospels, were included in this work—John because he died of natural causes after being exiled to the island of Patmos, and Luke because he was not one of the twelve.

All the disciples witnessed Jesus' crucifixion, and all of them interacted with Him after His resurrection. Upon His resurrection, graves opened, and hundreds of the dead arose.

[52] "and the tombs broke open. The bodies of many holy people who had died were raised to life. [53] They came out of the tombs after Jesus' resurrection and went into the holy city and appeared to many people" (**Matthew 27:52-53 (NIV).**

You have now read descriptions of the deaths of fourteen of Jesus' companions. Now I will share with you how Jesus died but first you may wonder who wanted him dead and why.

The who were the Jewish Religious and Social Leaders, the Pharisees and Sadducees and the why is because he claimed to be God and exposed their hypocritic practices in front of the huge crowds.

CONSIDER THESE VERSES FROM THE MESSAGE BIBLE (MSG) IN THE BOOK OF MATTHEW 23: 1-39:

[1-3] Now Jesus turned to address his disciples, along with the crowd that had gathered with them. "The religion scholars and Pharisees are competent teachers in God's Law. You won't go wrong in following their teachings on Moses. But be careful about following them. They talk a good line, but they don't live it. They don't take it into their hearts and live it out in their behavior. It's all spit-and-polish veneer.

[4-7] "Instead of giving you God's Law as food and drink by which you can banquet on God, they package it in bundles of rules, loading you down like pack animals. They seem to take pleasure in watching you stagger under these loads, and wouldn't think of lifting a finger to help. Their lives are perpetual fashion shows, embroidered prayer shawls one day and flowery prayers the next. They love to sit at the head table at church dinners, basking in the most prominent positions, preening in the radiance of public flattery, receiving honorary degrees, and getting called 'Doctor' and 'Reverend.'

[8-10] "Don't let people do that to you, put you on a pedestal like that. You all have a single Teacher, and you are all classmates. Don't set people up as experts over your life, letting them tell you what to do. Save that authority for God; let him tell you what to do. No one else should carry the title of 'Father'; you have only one Father, and he's in heaven. And don't let people maneuver you into taking charge of them. There is only one Life-Leader for you and them—Christ.

[11-12] "Do you want to stand out? Then step down. Be a servant. If you puff yourself up, you'll get the wind knocked out of you. But if you're content to simply be yourself, your life will count for plenty.

Frauds!

[13] "I've had it with you! You're hopeless, you religion scholars, you Pharisees! Frauds! Your lives are roadblocks to God's kingdom. You refuse to enter, and won't let anyone else in either.

[15] "You're hopeless, you religion scholars and Pharisees! Frauds!

You go halfway around the world to make a convert, but once you get him you make him into a replica of yourselves, double-damned.

16-22 "You're hopeless! What arrogant stupidity! You say, 'If someone makes a promise with his fingers crossed, that's nothing; but if he swears with his hand on the Bible, that's serious.' What ignorance! Does the leather on the Bible carry more weight than the skin on your hands? And what about this piece of trivia: 'If you shake hands on a promise, that's nothing; but if you raise your hand that God is your witness, that's serious'? What ridiculous hairsplitting! What difference does it make whether you shake hands or raise hands? A promise is a promise. What difference does it make if you make your promise inside or outside a house of worship? A promise is a promise. God is present, watching and holding you to account regardless.

23-24 "You're hopeless, you religion scholars and Pharisees! Frauds! You keep meticulous account books, tithing on every nickel and dime you get, but on the meat of God's Law, things like fairness and compassion and commitment—the absolute basics!—you carelessly take it or leave it. Careful bookkeeping is commendable, but the basics are required. Do you have any idea how silly you look, writing a life story that's wrong from start to finish, nitpicking over commas and semicolons?

25-26 "You're hopeless, you religion scholars and Pharisees! Frauds! You buff the surface of your cups and bowls so they sparkle in the sun, while the insides are maggoty with your greed and gluttony. Stupid Pharisee! Scour the insides, and then the gleaming surface will mean something.

27-28 "You're hopeless, you religion scholars and Pharisees! Frauds! You're like manicured grave plots, grass clipped and flowers bright, but six feet down, it's all rotting bones and worm-eaten flesh. People look at you and think you're saints, but beneath the skin, you're total frauds.

29-32 "You're hopeless, you religion scholars and Pharisees! Frauds! You build granite tombs for your prophets and marble monuments

81

for your saints. And you say that if you had lived in the days of your ancestors, no blood would have been on your hands. You protest too much! You're cut from the same cloth as those murderers, and daily add to the death count.

[33-34] "Snakes! Cold-blooded sneaks! Do you think you can worm your way out of this? Never have to pay the piper? It's on account of people like you that I send prophets and wise guides and scholars generation after generation—and generation after generation, you treat them like dirt, greeting them with lynch mobs, hounding them with abuse.

[35-36] "You can't squirm out of this: Every drop of righteous blood ever spilled on this earth, beginning with the blood of that good man Abel right down to the blood of Zechariah, Barachiah's son, whom you murdered at his prayers, is on your head. All this, I'm telling you, is coming down on you, on your generation. town. What is there left to say? Only this: I'm out of here soon. The next time you see me, you'll say, 'Oh, God has blessed him! He's come, bringing God's rule!'

[37-39] "Jerusalem! Jerusalem! Murderer of prophets! Killer of the ones who brought you God's news! How often I've ached to embrace your children, the way a hen gathers her chicks under her wings, and you wouldn't let me. And now you're so desolate, nothing but a ghost town. What is there left to say? Only this: I'm out of here soon. The next time you see me you'll say, 'Oh, God has blessed him! He's come, bringing God's rule!'"

This was his final speech before the conspiracy to kill him was carried out. Jesus was arrested and taken before the Jewish Court, the Sanhedrin and the High Priest Caiaphas. There it is believed he was mocked, spit upon and punched repeatedly.

He was then taken to the Roman Officials, Pilate and Herod. Herod refused to be involved because he sensed that the whole conspiracy was a sham and smartly did not want Jesus' blood on his hands. It is believed that Pilate ordered Jesus' scourging. The scourging was carried out using a flagrum, a whip with a wooden handle that has leather thongs that have heavy metal balls

82

attached to them. Jesus was beaten with this until he was unrecognizable, sliced to the bone, his tissue shredded and arteries, blood vessels gushing blood from everywhere.

Virtually dead, he was nailed to a cross with large square nails through his wrists and feet, and a crown of thorns was pressed through his scalp against his skull, causing even more bleeding. Excruciating pain, either from supporting his weight with his feet or arms, was constant.

He pushed down at least seven times on his feet while pulling up with his arms in order to get a breath of air, each time he spoke.

His first words were, "Father forgive them for they know not what they do."

Then to the repentant criminal, "Today, thou shalt be with me in paradise."

The third time that he strained for a breath, he spoke to his Brother John and said, "Behold thy mother," and to mother Mary, "Woman, behold thy son."

Again, he got a breath and cried out to God, "My God, My God, why hast thou forsaken me?"

A fifth time, he struggled for a small breath of air and said, "I thirst."

Near death, he said, "It is finished."

And at last, he spoke his last words, "Father, into thy hands I commit my spirit."

Unable to support himself, slumping down, he could no longer breathe properly. Modern doctors suspect that Jesus did not suffocate but likely died due to massive blood loss, shock, and heart failure.

Consider this, Scientists and Religious Types have been at odds for eons, attempting to answer life's biggest questions:

Where did we come from?

Who are we?

What are we supposed to do?

Where are we going/What will happen to us when we die?

The Scientists/Evolutionists believe that from some unknown source a single cell decided to mutate and over millions or billions of years somehow morphed from a non-breathing blind, deaf, mute thing became something else and eventually mutated enough times that people, dogs, cats, cows, fish, birds, snakes.... are the results of this evolutionary process.

Oh yes, don't forget that this single cell became fruits, vegetables, herbs, and everything humans need to sustain life. Sadly, there are no fossils identifying the transitional forms that are evolutionary.

There is no missing link, there is no monkey or Ape man. Darwin admitted that if the missing link couldn't be found, all his thoughts and work was for naught.

Don't get me wrong, scientists using our five senses (*Sense Knowledge*), seeing, tasting, hearing, smelling, and feeling, have proven and invented astonishing things that improve and save lives and bring great comfort and pleasure to us all. Flight, medicine, electricity, cars, music, heat, and air conditioning are a tiny sample of what can be done just using our five senses. *Sense Knowledge* is amazing, but it is limited. It does not answer the four big questions of life.

> *Where did we come from?*
>
> *Who are we?*
>
> *What are we supposed to do?*
>
> *Where are we going/What will happen to us when we die*

Nor can it explain, prove or understand the human spirit. It can't define what the source is. It has no explanation for who or what God is. It has not proven the origin of matter, life, or creation.

Let's consider the Biblical World View, can it answer the four questions?

Where did we come from?

Genesis 1:1-5 (KJV)

84

[1] In the beginning God created the heaven and the earth.

[2] And the earth was without form, and void; and darkness was upon the face of the deep. And the Spirit of God moved upon the face of the waters.

[3] And God said, Let there be light: and there was light.

[4] And God saw the light, that it was good: and God divided the light from the darkness.

[5] And God called the light Day, and the darkness he called Night. And the evening and the morning were the first day.

Who are we?

Genesis 1:26-27 (KJV)

[26] And God said, Let us make man in our image, after our likeness: and let them have dominion over the fish of the sea, and over the fowl of the air, and over the cattle, and over all the earth, and over every creeping thing that creepeth upon the earth.

[27] So God created man in his own image, in the image of God created he him; male and female created he them.

What are we supposed to do?

Genesis 1: 28-31 (KJV)

[28] And God blessed them, and God said unto them, Be fruitful, and multiply, and replenish the earth, and

subdue it: and have dominion over the fish of the sea, and over the fowl of the air, and over every living thing that moveth upon the earth.

[29] And God said, Behold, I have given you every herb bearing seed, which is upon the face of all the earth, and every tree, in the which is the fruit of a tree yielding seed; to you it shall be for meat.

[30] And to every beast of the earth, and to every fowl of the air, and to every thing that creepeth upon the earth, wherein there is life, I have given every green herb for meat: and it was so.

[31] And God saw every thing that he had made, and, behold, it was very good. And the evening and the morning were the sixth day.

Matthew 28: 16-20 (KJV)

[16] Then the eleven disciples went away into Galilee, into a mountain where Jesus had appointed them. [17] And when they saw him, they worshipped him: but some doubted.

[18] And Jesus came and spake unto them, saying, All power is given unto me in heaven and in earth.

[19] Go ye therefore, and teach all nations, baptizing them in the name of the Father, and of the Son, and of the Holy Ghost:

[20] Teaching them to observe all things whatsoever I have commanded you: and, lo, I am with you always,

even unto the end of the world. Amen.

Where are we going/What will happen to us when we die?

You get to choose!

2 Peter 3:9 (ESV)

"The Lord is not slow to fulfill his promise as some count slowness, but is patient toward you, not wishing that any should perish, but that all should reach repentance."

John 3:16 (ESV)

"For God so loved the world, that he gave his only Son, that whoever believes in him should not perish but have eternal life."

2 Timothy 2:4 (ESV)

"No soldier gets entangled in civilian pursuits, since his aim is to please the one who enlisted him."

John 6:40 (ESV)

"For this is the will of my Father, that everyone who looks on the Son and believes in him should have eternal life, and I will raise him up on the last day."

Romans 10:13 (ESV)

"For everyone who calls on the name of the Lord will be saved."

87

Romans 5:8 (ESV)

"But God shows his love for us in that while we were still sinners, Christ died for us."

Romans 6:23 (ESV)

"For the wages of sin is death, but the free gift of God is eternal life in Christ Jesus our Lord."

John 1:12 (ESV)

"But to all who did receive him, who believed in his name, he gave the right to become children of God."

John 5:24 (ESV)

"Truly, truly, I say to you, whoever hears my word and believes him who sent me has eternal life. He does not come into judgment but has passed from death to life."

John 14:6 (ESV)

"Jesus said to him, '*I am the way, and the truth, and the life. No one comes to the Father except through me.*'"

Romans 3:23 (ESV)

"For all have sinned and fall short of the glory of God."

Romans 10:9 (ESV)

"Because, if you confess with your mouth that Jesus is Lord and believe in your heart that God raised him from the dead, you will be saved."

Ephesians 2:8-9 (ESV)

"For by grace you have been saved through faith. And this is not your own doing; it is the gift of God, not a result of works, so that no one may boast."

So why hasn't religion worked for you? You probably experienced exactly what Jesus said to the Sadducees and Pharisees in Matthew 23:1-39.

Woe, woe, woe...

Believe it or not, the scientists (*Sense Knowledge*) in many cases have taken over the church and theological schools (seminaries). Many churches and denominations have ceased being spiritual bodies. Sense knowledge—because it can't prove them—will deny answered prayer, miracles, and the inerrancy of the Bible and the deity of Jesus Christ.

Yes, it is possible that churchgoers, the "religious," don't believe in miracles, healing, or God's supernatural power. Yes—unbelievable, I know.

Consider this quote by Adam Kirsch: [3]

The best atheists agree with the best defenders of faith (in God) on one crucial point: That choice to believe or disbelieve is existentially the most important choice of all. It shapes one's whole understanding of human life and purpose, because it is a choice that each must make for him or herself.

Answering the questions:

Who am I?

Where did I come from?

What am I supposed to do?

And where am I going when I die?

---

[3] Excerpt paraphrased from Adam Kirsch's commentary on faith and meaning. Original works available at *The New York Times* and *Tablet Magazine*.

89

...are challenging questions each of us should answer. In the end, it is important to know whether God exists, or He does not exist. There is no third option.

If the evidence you have just read has caused you to believe that the bestselling book of all time, "The Bible," is true, and you would like to become a follower of Jesus, like the fourteen martyrs you just met, you need only to pray a simple prayer, something like this:

Dear God, please forgive me.

For whatever reason, up until right now, I have been confused, not believed, or have been opposed to you, Jesus, and the whole Bible story. I repent and want to be your follower.

I believe that Jesus is Your only begotten son, that He died on the cross for my sins, that He descended to hell but arose three days later in full life.

I believe I am healed by the stripes that He took on my behalf, that His sacrifice of His body and blood has paid the full debt for my sin.

I believe that upon my physical death, my spirit will live forever in heaven with You.

Please just pray, as your spirit directs you.

Please call the Billy Graham hotline at 1-855-255-7729 to let them know about your decision and to receive information on how you move forward with your newfound faith—Peace be with you.

90

THE DIFFERENCE BETWEEN A DISCIPLE AND A FOLLOWER

"A disciple is not above his teacher. But everyone, when he is fully trained will be like his teacher."

— JESUS (LUKE 6:40 ESV)

As we conclude this journey through the lives and lessons of Jesus' disciples, let's take a moment to reflect on what set them apart from the crowds that followed Him. Many people followed Jesus to witness His miracles or seek food and healing, but there's no evidence that their commitment went beyond the immediate. His disciples, on the other hand, were called to leave their old lives behind and devote themselves fully to spreading His teachings and ministering to others.

This alone takes a brave person: To give up everything you know and devote yourself to a single cause is a sure mark of dedication and belief, and each of the men we're looking at here had it in droves.

Their mission was to carry Jesus' message as far as they could, connecting people to God and to each other. Indeed, this is how the Word of God has spread throughout history—through sharing faith with others and guiding them to follow in the footsteps of Jesus—and the disciples were the first people dedicated to this noble cause.

Just as they spread Jesus' message, you can help other people learn more about these brave men and deepen their understanding of Jesus and His teachings—and doing so will cost you far less effort than it cost them. All you need to do is leave a few words online.

By leaving a review of this book on Amazon, you'll raise awareness about the disciples and show new readers where they can find out more about the important work they did.

Just like word of mouth, reviews are a powerful way to share knowledge. By sharing your review, you'll play a part in spreading the disciples' legacy and Jesus' message to even more people.

Thank you so much for your support. Your words make a difference!

ORDER OF DISCIPLES CALLED BY JESUS

1. Simon Peter

2. Andrew

3. James, son of Zebedee

4. John

5. Philip

6. Bartholomew

7. Thomas

8. Matthew

9. James, son of Alphaeus

10. Thaddaeus

11. Simon the Zealot

12. Judas Iscariot

DISCIPLES WHO WERE BROTHERS

Peter and Andrew—Sons of Jonah James and John—Sons of Zebedee.

THIRTY-SEVEN MIRACLES OF JESUS IN CHRONOLOGICAL ORDER

Thirty-Seven Miracles of Jesus in Chronological Order					
#	Miracle	Matthew	Mark	Luke	John
1	Jesus Turns Water into Wine at the Wedding in Cana				2:1-11
2	Jesus Heals an Official's Son at Capernaum in Galilee				4:43-54
3	Jesus Drives Out an Evil Spirit from a Man in Capernaum		1:21-27	4:31-36	
4	Jesus Heals Peter's Mother-in-Law Sick with Fever	8:14-15	1:29-31	4:38-39	
5	Jesus Heals Many Sick and Oppressed at Evening	8:16-17	1:32-34	4:40-41	
6	First Miraculous Catch of Fish on the Lake of Gennesaret			5:1-11	
7	Jesus Cleanses a Man with Leprosy	8:1-4	1:40-45	5:12-14	
8	Jesus Heals a Centurion's Paralyzed Servant in Capernaum	8:5-13		7:1-10	
9	Jesus Heals a Paralytic Who Was Let Down from the Roof	9:1-8	2:1-12	5:17-26	
10	Jesus Heals a Man's Withered Hand on the Sabbath	12:9-14	3:1-6	6:6-11	
11	Jesus Raises a Widow's Son from the Dead in Nain			7:11-17	

12	Jesus Calms a Storm on the Sea	8:23, 27-32	4:45-41	8:22-25	
13	Jesus Casts Demons into a Herd of Pigs	8:28-33	5:1-20	8:26-39	
14	Jesus Heals a Woman in the Crowd with an Issue of Blood	9:20-22	5:25-34	8:42-48	
15	Jesus Raises Jairus' Daughter Back to Life	9:18, 23-26	5:21-24, 35-43	8:40-42, 49-56	
16	Jesus Heals Two Blind Men	9:27-31			
17	Jesus Heals a Man Who Was Unable to Speak	9:32-34			
18	Jesus Heals an Invalid at Bethesda				5:1-15
19	Jesus Feeds 5,000 Plus Women and Children	14:13-21	6:30-44	9:10-17	6:1-15
20	Jesus Walks on Water	14:22-33	6:45-52		6:16-21
21	Jesus Heals Many Sick in Gennesaret as They Touch His Garment	14:34-36	6:53-56		
22	Jesus Heals a Gentile Woman's Demon-Possessed Daughter	15:21-28	7:24-30		
23	Jesus Heals a Deaf and Dumb Man		7:31-37		
24	Jesus Feeds 4,000 Plus Women and Children	15:32-39	8:1-13		
25	Jesus Heals a Blind Man at Bethsaida		8:22-26		
26	Jesus Heals a Man Born Blind by Spitting in His Eyes				9:1-12

95

27	Jesus Heals a Boy with an Unclean Spirit	17:14-20	9:14-29	9:37-43	
28	Miraculous Temple Tax in a Fish's Mouth	17:24-27			
29	Jesus Heals a Blind, Mute Demoniac	12:22-23		11:14-23	
30	Jesus Heals a Woman Who Had Been Crippled for Eighteen Years			13:10-17	
31	Jesus Heals a Man with Dropsy on the Sabbath			14:1-6	
32	Jesus Cleanses Ten Lepers on the Way to Jerusalem			17:11-19	
33	Jesus Raises Lazarus from the Dead in Bethany				11:1-45
34	Jesus Restores Sight to Bartimaeus in Jericho	20:29-34	10:46-52	18:35-43	
35	Jesus Withers the Fig Tree on the Road from Bethany	21:18:22	11:12-14		
36	Jesus Heals a Servant's Severed Ear While He Is Being Arrested			22:50-51	
37	The Second Miraculous Catch of Fish at the Sea of Tiberias				21:4-11

REFERENCES

Global Disciples Canada. "Inspiring Discipleship Quotes: Gateway to a Life of Faith." *Global Disciples Canada.* Last modified January 8, 2024. https://www.globaldisciples.ca/blog/inspiring-discipleship-quotes-gateway-to-a-life-of-faith/

Strathearn, Gaye. "Why Being a Disciple is More Than Just Being a Follower." *Church News.* Last modified January 10, 2024. https://www.thechurchnews.com/living-faith/2022/12/28/23528416/being-a-disciple-is-more-than-just-being-a-follower-jesus-christ-gaye-strathearn/

Davis, C. Truman, M.D. "A Physician's View of the Crucifixion of Jesus Christ." *CBN.* December 10, 2022. https://cbn.com/article/suffering/physicians-view-crucifixion-jesus-christ

Kenyon, E. W. *Jesus the Healer.* Whitaker House. Published by Royal Christian Bookstores & Cafés, July 14, 2020. https://www.royalchristianbookstores.com/jesus-healer

Kirsch, Adam. "Why Do We Believe?" *Tablet Magazine.* Accessed [insert access date]. https://www.tabletmag.com/sections/belief/articles/why-do-we-believe.

Foxe, John. *Foxe: Voices of the Martyrs.* Salem Books, October 8, 2019. https://secure.persecution.com/p-7035-foxe-voices-of-the-martyrs.aspx

B&H Publishing Group. *Cornerstone Ultra-Thin Reference Bible.* Nashville, TN: B&H Publishing, 1999.

Simmons III, Richard E. *Reflections on the Existence of God.* Union Hill Publishing, December 14, 2019. https://richardesimmons3.com/product/reflections-on-the-existence-of-god/

Made in the USA
Columbia, SC
29 July 2025

61042676R00055